THAT'S A GOOD Question!

CHAPTER 1 GOD AND THE BIBLE 4

CHAPTER 2 ORIGINS 8

CHAPTER 3 PUZZLES ABOUT GOD AND HEAVEN 20

CHAPTER 4 PUZZLES ABOUT JESUS 40

CHAPTER 5 PUZZLES OF LIFE 48

CHAPTER 6 HOW SHOULD I LIVE? 56

J.Jo.

Illustrated by Tom Tinn-Disbury

I think asking questions is good.

That is how we learn. We are **curious!**
Over the years people have asked questions
like: "Why does it get dark at night?",
"What caused that rash?" or even
"Would putting pineapple on pizza taste nice?"
That's how we got science, doctors, cooking and
all sorts of good things. All the following questions
were given to me by children and I have enjoyed
trying to answer them. I hope you will also enjoy
reading both the questions and the answers.

CHAPTER 1

How do we know the Bible is true?

Well, I think for me there are two reasons.

The first reason is to do with facts. The fact is that the Bible is one of the most unique books in existence. It's not a book written by one person at one time but a collection of little books written by many people from different countries speaking different languages over a period of nearly 2,000 years.

It's a bit like St Paul's Cathedral in London. It was designed by one man named Christopher Wren, but his design was put together by thousands of skilled workers. These different men and women built the cathedral but they built it in line with the direction, guidance and master plan of Sir Christopher Wren. It is both his work and their work. So it is with the Bible. It's the work of lots of different people who were guided, inspired and directed by God. And everything we find in the pages of the Bible is written according to the master plan of God.

It's God's words written by men and women, which gives it authority.

The second reason is to do with feelings. I'm one of the millions of people who feel that the Bible speaks to us in a way that no other book does. Many people have started to read the Bible and sensed deep down that God is speaking directly to them through it. It's like when you get a letter or an email from a friend; even though they live miles away, when you read it you feel as if they are there with you. The Bible is like that, and it's a letter not just from a friend but from God.

How do we know God is real?

Some people say they don't believe in God because they can't see him but that doesn't worry me.

The fact is that there are all sorts of things that we can't see but everybody knows are real. For example, we can't see love but we know it's real. Or when we blow up a balloon we can't see the air but we know it exists.

"Just like air, God is there."

He never asks us to just guess that he exists. Even though we can't see him, he's left us a lot of evidence that we can see so we know he's real. For example, he's left us clues in how he created the world. I look around and it seems to me that the world didn't just happen but that someone made it, and that someone is God. I can't prove that but when I look at flowers, sunsets, stars and babies, that's what it looks like to me.

Second, I know many people who are full of love, joy and peace, and they tell me that they are like that because God changed their lives. And God has changed my life. I didn't always believe in him but when I became a follower of Jesus, he became real to me. Now, I think that's very important. After all, if God was imaginary you wouldn't expect anybody's life to be changed by him. Only real things change lives.

CHAPTER 2
ORIGINS

How old is God?

When was God born?

The only information that we can trust about God is what he has told us about himself in the Bible. And there God clearly says that he is "eternal", which means he never had a beginning and will never have an end.

That is hard for us to understand, but it's true. In fact the Bible says that to God a thousand years can be just like a day. Time doesn't mean the same thing to God as it does to us.

In the Bible we read: "Before the mountains were born, before you gave birth to the Earth and the world, from beginning to end, you are God." In other words, God is older than the entire universe.

God is someone who always was, always is and always will be. He wasn't born; he wasn't made; he just is. No, I can't get my head around it either but there are a lot of things in life that we can't fully understand. The good news about this is that we trust God for our whole life because, as the Bible says, he is the same yesterday, today and forever. So he's not going to change. Ever. And that is really good to know.

When did God make Adam and Eve?

The Bible tells us that God made human beings special and that he called the first humans "Adam" and "Eve" and that all other human beings have come from them.

Now the Bible doesn't tell us when these things happened but it was a very long time ago. The Bible doesn't tell us all we would like to know but it tells us all we need to know. After all, when you are ill doctors don't give you all the details of how your insides actually work; they simply give you something to make you better.

The story of Adam and Eve is important.

For one thing it tells us that everybody we meet comes from the same great, great, great, great - and so on almost forever - grandparents. In other words, whatever we look like, whatever colour our skin is, whether we are young or old, we are all human. That means that everybody is equally valuable and we should treat everybody as being as important as ourselves.

Adam & Eve

Why do people have different colour skin if we are all descended from Adam and Eve?

Here I had to do some research.

Scientists who study how the human body works have discovered that we need just the right amount of sunlight to go through our skin.

If we get too little sunlight going through we don't get enough of something really important called Vitamin D. On the other hand, if we get too much sunlight going through then there is a risk of getting some very nasty skin diseases.

So as human beings spread out all over the Earth over many thousands of years, their skin colour changed to allow them to get just the right amount of sunlight.

Those people near the equator where there is a lot of strong sunlight got darker skins and those people in areas far away from the equator, where the sun is much weaker, got pale skins. Clever, eh?

So that's the science reason.

Personally, I think
there's another reason
which is that God likes variety. The really
important thing is that having a different colour
skin really doesn't matter; it's what you are deep
down inside that matters.

13

Why did God create the world?

To be honest we don't know why God created the world but, in my opinion, it's because God is like an artist. And just as people paint pictures or create music to say something about who they are, I believe that God made the world, the stars, plants and animals, and absolutely everything, to show us, in some way, who he is.

When we look at everything around us we see how powerful, creative and amazing God is.

Why did God make people?

Another good question - actually two questions. If you talk to people who paint pictures, write books or make music, they will often say about what they have made: "I put something of myself into that." And when God made people he made them to show, in some way, a little bit of who he is. God likes making things; that's just who he is.

Was God lonely?

Now, for your second question. No, God wasn't lonely. The reason is because the Bible says that although there is only one God, he is also three. There is God the Father, God the Son (that's Jesus) and God the Holy Spirit, and they are all in the one God. Now even if you struggle to understand what that means – and everybody does – it does tell us that long before people were created, God would have been able to have someone to talk to.

Were there dinosaurs on the ark?

I have to admit it's a great idea.

Can you imagine it? A big boat full of animals with dinosaurs the size of a double-decker bus. Not to mention a storm going on outside. But it seems that the dinosaurs died out before the great flood, so probably not.

It is important to always remember that the Bible is not a science textbook but the story of God's plan and purpose for people, like you and me. And it doesn't say anything about dinosaurs.

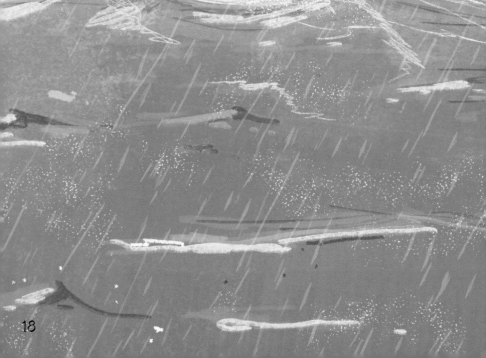

CHAPTER 3
PUZZLES ABOUT GOD AND HEAVEN

What does God look like?

Okay, let me begin by telling you what God doesn't look like. He doesn't look like an old man with a beard sitting on a cloud. That's cartoon stuff!

The truth is much more interesting. In one way, it's true to say that we can never see God. It's not only that he is invisible but if we could see him we would be in big trouble.

God is so perfect and powerful and dazzling that we would be, well, fried. Yet although we can't really see God now, in the Bible we are told that Jesus Christ "is the visible image of the invisible God". As someone said, "Jesus is God with skin on." In fact Jesus himself said that anyone who had seen him had seen God the Father.

Actually, the big issue with God is not what he looks like but what he is like as a person: he is good and loving. The best way to think about what God looks like is to think of him as being like Jesus.

The WORLD's WORST
GOD IMPERSONATORS

21

Where does God live?

God is everywhere.

He sees everything, knows everything and keeps everything going.

Sometimes we think of God as though he were another person like us. And just as we can only be in one place at a time and we need a place to live, we think that God is the same. But God isn't limited to a physical body or to one place at a time.

In fact God lives inside people who love him. We call church "God's house" because that's where people who love God gather together to worship him.

But no matter where we are, God is with us. He is keeping the most distant star going but at the same time he is also keeping a loving eye on you and me.

HERE

God can answer the prayer from a girl in China while comforting you when you're sad. He listens to our praise in church, but he also watches how we act on the playground. God is with us wherever we go, so we can be sure that he is always watching and caring for us.

Now some people don't like the idea of God being constantly around them. But if you have become a friend of God through knowing Jesus then the idea that he's watching over you is wonderful. Mind you, don't be silly. Just because God is watching over you doesn't mean to say that you can take risks. It's still a good idea to be very careful when you do things like cross the road.

Does God sleep?

Definitely not.

I mean the idea that God might sleep is, well, worrying enough to keep you awake at night. After all, he manages the whole universe, from slugs to stars. Just think, if God was to close his eyes and fall asleep anything could happen!

Thankfully, God doesn't sleep. God does not have a physical body like us, so he doesn't need to sleep or eat.

When the Bible says "God rests" it means he has stopped doing something. But God doesn't get tired or worn out, so he doesn't need to rest the way we do.

The Bible clearly tells us that God watches over his people and that not only does he not sleep, he doesn't even get sleepy.

Actually, there's a story about this.

A long time ago, in the Second World War, planes regularly bombed London at night. Someone met a woman who lived close to where the bombs were falling and was surprised at how well she looked. So he asked her, "Aren't you kept awake at night by fear and worry?"

"Oh, I sleep just fine," she replied. "I read in the Bible that God doesn't sleep so I decided that there was no point in both of us staying awake."

That's good thinking. God watches over all of us day and night.

Who made God?

A lot of smart people have asked this question. After all, if everything has a beginning or is made out of something or had a creator, then people think God must have had one too!

Let's think about it. If someone made God, then you must have a bigger God who made that God . . . and a bigger, bigger God who made that bigger God who made God . . . then a bigger, bigger, bigger God who made the bigger, bigger God who made the bigger God who made God. You see, we could go on and on and on.

The answer to this is easy to give, but hard to understand. Are you ready? Good. Well nobody created God; he always was. There was never a time when God did not exist. You see, part of the problem here is that we think that God is like us. But he isn't. Perhaps the best way to explain this is to think of cartoons.

Yes, really. Imagine my son Ben draws a famous cartoon character on a sheet of paper. For us human beings to ask, "Who made God?" is a little bit like the cartoon character asking, "Who drew Ben?" That question doesn't make a lot of sense, does it? I think asking, "Who made God?" is pretty similar.

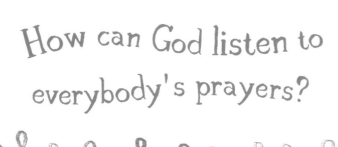

How can God listen to everybody's prayers?

The thing is that God is so much bigger and greater than we can imagine. He is everywhere and he's capable of seeing everything all the time.

God can hear everyone's prayers at once because God is everywhere. We can only be in one place at a time, and usually we can't understand more than one person at a time. Not only can God hear and understand everyone who is praying to him in many different languages, but he can also give each person his full attention.

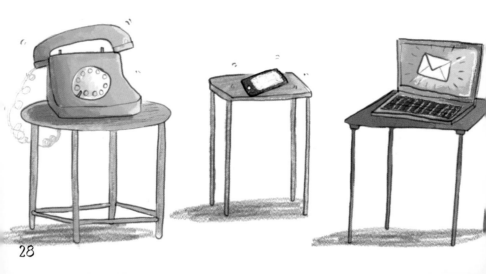

Free Phone
God on
1234-GOD-89

You must have seen things on the television or computer where everything goes really . . . really . . . s - l - o - w - l - y because they have done clever things with the camera and the film is in slow motion. Well I guess that God can probably do that with everything.

So if there are a lot of prayers coming in - no problem. God just slows down everything to give everybody the opportunity to be heard.

But it's a great thing to realise that God never says, "Sorry, I'm too busy to listen to your prayers right now. Can you call me back?" The fact is God does listen to everybody's prayers. In the Bible it says, "When you pray, I will listen."

Does God know when I've done something wrong?

Yes, he does.

Even if you are deep underground, far out in space, wearing a disguise or just simply hiding under your bed, God sees everything. In the Bible we read: "The LORD is watching everywhere, keeping his eye on both the evil and the good."

So yes, he does know when we've done something wrong. But because he is a God who loves us he will forgive us if we come to him and say we are sorry.

Whatever the issue, he already knows about it and wants us to feel safe enough to tell him our thoughts.

God knows our thoughts, and he helps us to know ourselves better when we talk them over with him.

Does God know what I'm thinking?

Yes, he does.

The Bible tells us that God knows exactly what we are thinking.

For instance, in one of the Psalms we read this about God: "You know when I sit down or stand up. You know my thoughts even when I'm far away."

Now this might seem embarrassing because thoughts are the most private part of us, but it's really rather important. I think it's good that God knows when we are frightened or nervous. It also means that God is never fooled by appearances. You see, we often meet people who seem very pleasant and come out with nice words, but later on we find that, beneath the surface, they were really thinking and planning bad things. God isn't fooled that way because he knows what's in everybody's minds.

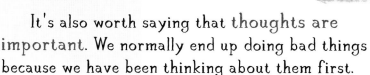

It's also worth saying that thoughts are important. We normally end up doing bad things because we have been thinking about them first.

To let yourself think about things in a wrong way is to plant seeds in your mind which can sprout up into bad actions. In fact Jesus said that wanting to do something wrong is like doing the wrong thing. So wishing you could hit someone is actually not much better than hitting them. We should try not to think bad thoughts and ask Jesus to help us keep our thoughts good and clean.

OPEN

BUS STOP

Where is heaven?

The reality is that heaven – the place where God is – is all around us but we just can't see it. It's just invisible at the moment. That is because it is hidden from our eyes, but not from our hearts. We are limited human beings. We can't even get off this planet without a rocket. But he is the unlimited God of heaven and can be anywhere, all at once. He is very big, and very wonderful.

Let me have a go at explaining it.

First of all, imagine your favourite computer game or television programme. Now think of your favourite character in it and imagine that he or she (or it) can think the way we can. That would be strange. After all, they would think that their world was real and it was all that there was. They couldn't possibly imagine that, all around them, our world existed and that it was much greater, much more solid and more wonderful than theirs.

I think that heaven is like that. Heaven is the "world beyond our world" and it's actually more solid and real than this world and it's also going to last for ever.

The thing is that even if we don't understand where heaven is, what we always need to remember is that God and heaven are always close to us. Knowing that can help us when we are in trouble, when we are frightened or sad, or when we are tempted to do things that are wrong.

What is heaven like?

The truth is that while we don't really know what heaven is like, we do know that it's going to be fantastic.

First, because God is going to be at the centre of heaven and he is pure goodness, no bad or evil things can be there. In fact we are told that in heaven "there will be no more death or sorrow or crying or pain. All these things are gone forever". We won't need tissues or medicine. We won't need doctors, police or soldiers. No wars. There won't be any swords, spears, guns or bombs. How good is that!

Welcome to
HEAVEN
"The city of gold"

Second, not only will heaven be empty of bad things, it will be full of good things. There will be fun, joy, love and laughter. That may sound like a party to you and, actually, when Jesus talked about heaven that's exactly how he described it. In heaven we will get new bodies. Our bodies will never get tired or sick. Our bodies will never break or die.

Finally, one of the best things about heaven is that it goes on for ever. Heaven never ends. And we will never want it to end because in heaven we get to see God face to face and enjoy him for ever.

And that's the best part about heaven. You see, one of the problems with good things in this life is that they have to end. But the great thing about heaven is that it will never ever end.

37

How do we get into heaven?

Now here's something important that a lot of people get wrong. You and I can't get into heaven because of what we have done.

You can try to be absolutely perfect in all that you do, what you say and even what you think, but it's never going to be good enough. Heaven is a perfect place and only perfect people get in. So actually, of all the people that have ever lived, the only person who could ever get in to heaven by what they had done is Jesus because he was perfect.

Now that may not seem good news for the rest of us but, trust me, it is. You see, to let Jesus come into your heart through God's Holy Spirit is to become part of his family. Without God sending Jesus to Earth to die for us, there would be no way for us to get to heaven. That's the good news of Jesus: God made a way for everyone. And Jesus is the way.

Imagine there's a long queue of people waiting to go to the cinema and in the queue is a parent. When they get to the entrance, they present a ticket to the person standing there. "You are welcome," says the person at the door, "come on in!"

"Thank you," says the parent, "but did you notice that it's a family ticket?" and then they turn around and wave on in a whole lot of children who are part of their family.

You see, to follow Jesus is to become a child of God and a member of his family, and that's how we get into heaven. So what do you need to do to get into heaven? Pray to Jesus, admit that you have done wrong things, ask to be forgiven, invite Jesus into your life and follow him from now on.

39

CHAPTER 4   PUZZLES ABOUT JESUS

Why did Jesus come to Earth?

I can think of three reasons why Jesus came.

The **first** reason is Jesus came to show us what God is like. It's a bit like science in school where teachers will tell you about something in words and it makes a bit of sense, but then they show you a demonstration and that makes it all so much more real.

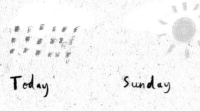

In Jesus, the God who is invisible became visible. It's as if God was saying, "Look, there are all sorts of ideas about what I am like: let me show you!"

The second reason is that Jesus became one of us to show us what we should be like. Jesus was kind and caring, spoke the truth, loved God in every way, loved all people and did nothing that was wrong.

The third reason is that God had to become one of us in order to set us free by paying the price for the things we have all done wrong. To be on our side Jesus had

to be born as one of us so that he could die as one of us.

Jesus came to save you. He loves you and wants to be a part of your life.

Was Jesus a man or God?

Name: Jesus
Place of Birth: Bethlehem
Grew up: Nazareth
God: 100%

Both. That's the easy bit; the tough bit is explaining what "both" means.

For 2,000 years the followers of Jesus have always said that they believe that Jesus was both a human being and God.

One way of thinking about this is to think of those sports games where you are allowed to have a substitute - someone who can be brought on into the game to take the place of someone else.

The Bible teaches that Jesus came to be our substitute and to take our place so that he could take our punishment.

Now in sport you can't just simply bring anybody on as a substitute, they have to have the right to do that; they have to be part of the team.

That's why God came to Earth as Jesus: there's only one way to become a member of "The Human Race" and that's to be human. "In Jesus, there is all of God in a human body."

The way I understand it is that if Jesus had been only a human being he could only have substituted for one other person. But if Jesus was God he could substitute for billions of people because he had infinite power.

So Jesus was a man so that he could have the right to save us, and he was God so that he could have the power to save us. That's why he was both man and God, and that's why there is no one else like him.

It also means that whatever we go through and whatever we do, Jesus can sympathise and relate to it. "Since he himself has gone through suffering and testing, he is able to help us when we are being tested."

Did Jesus rise from the dead?

This is the big question, isn't it? We all know, sometimes rather sadly, that dead things and dead people stay dead.

But the Bible says that, in his case, Jesus rose from the dead as someone who was so alive that, as it were, he overflowed with life.

Now the evidence for this is very good. The stories in the Gospels – Matthew, Mark, Luke and John – read like the records of what police call "eyewitness accounts".

And, however far you go back, the followers of Jesus always talked about him as being someone who, although he had died, was now alive.

FISH

The Bible tells us that all human beings die because we all do wrong things. Now that raises an interesting possibility. What would happen if there was someone who had done nothing wrong and they died?

It would make perfect sense that death would not be able to hold onto them: that they would, somehow, come back to life, like a piece of wood pushed down into water bobs back up to the surface. And I think something like that is what happened to Jesus.

The Bible says about Jesus: "But God released him from the horrors of death and raised him back to life, for death could not keep him in its grip." The fact that Jesus his risen from the dead is proof that he has defeated death for his followers and confirmed he had the power over death which no one could ignore.

How can Jesus fit in my heart?

You may have heard people say something like "Jesus came into my heart" and that can sound a bit weird. Someone might think it meant that they suddenly get a miniature Jesus bouncing around in their chest!

When people talk about "their heart" it doesn't always mean that really important bit of your body that pumps blood around.

When you or I talk about "my heart" we are often referring to what we feel deep down. So people say "I love you with all my heart" or "my heart sank". And when we use that way of speaking, the heart is very important because it refers to what we think, feel and do.

Someone talking about Jesus "coming into their heart" is saying how they invited Jesus to take over every part of their lives.

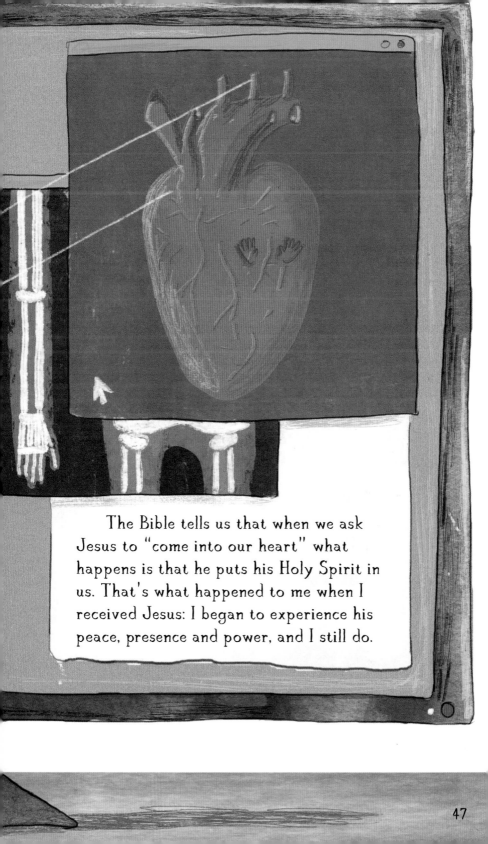

The Bible tells us that when we ask Jesus to "come into our heart" what happens is that he puts his Holy Spirit in us. That's what happened to me when I received Jesus: I began to experience his peace, presence and power, and I still do.

CHAPTER 5

Why does God let bad things happen?

This is one of the hardest questions in life to answer. Let me give you two wrong answers first.

Wrong answer number one is that bad things happen because God doesn't care. But that's wrong because the Bible tells us that God loves us so much that he sent his son Jesus to die for us.

Wrong answer number two is that bad things happen because God can't do anything about them. But that's wrong because God is all-powerful.

Actually, there is no simple right answer.

One answer is that bad things happen because people decided to disobey God and do things their way, not his. The result of this is that it's often our fault that the world is a bit of a mess and there are illnesses and accidents.

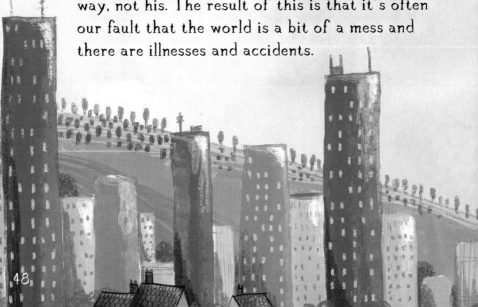

PUZZLES OF LIFE

For example, there is quite enough money in the world to make sure no one should starve or have to live near volcanoes that are going to erupt. But people like to keep money for themselves.

There is, however, good news: although God lets bad things happen now, he has promised that one day every bad thing will be stopped and God will take the world and make it into what it was originally meant to be.

Sometimes I think God lets bad things happen so that we will learn to trust him. It's also worth remembering that because God loves us he is sad when things go wrong for us.

Perhaps the most important thing about bad things is to not worry about what causes them but to live a life where we try to stop them from happening and help people who have suffered from bad things. Jesus cares when bad things happen. Jesus cried when his friend Lazarus died. The shortest verse in the Bible says: "Jesus wept."

Why do people die before they are old?

Death is the name we give to a very confusing part of life. We know that plants die in winter. We know that animals die too. We can understand that this is the way nature works. But it is much harder to understand why people die, especially someone we love.

The Bible is clear that dying is something that wasn't what God wanted for human beings. Death happened because human beings decided to disobey God and do what they wanted. The result of that disobedience is that people died.

In the Bible, however, we are promised that one day there will be a heaven for God's people in which there will be no more death. That's incredible!

In the meantime we all have to realise that our time on Earth is limited and the best thing to do is make the most of it by doing what God wants. God wants us to love him and to love other people. The big issue is not whether you live a long life or short life but whether you live the best life possible.

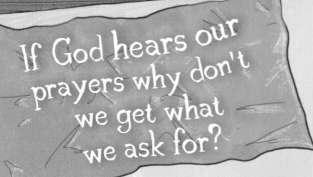

If God hears our prayers why don't we get what we ask for?

Good question.

The thing is that what we want and what is good for us are often two different things.

No one knows this better than parents who sometimes find themselves having to refuse to give their children what they want. For example, if you went up to your father and said, "Dad, for Christmas can I please have that mega box of chocolates that I've seen in the supermarket?"

it's quite likely that Dad might say, "No!" because he'd be concerned that you might be, well, mega sick.

And if someone came up to their mother and said, "Mum, can I watch all twelve episodes of this series in one go?" I would imagine that Mum is going to say, "No way!"

It's the same with our prayers: God loves us perfectly but he also knows us perfectly and he knows what will be good for us and what will be bad. So we have to trust him when he says no. There are lots of times when we pray to God and, as we do, we remind ourselves that "God loves me and he knows best".

PRETZEL CHOCOLATE

CARAMEL HEART

TRUFFLE STAR

CRISPY SWIRL

FUDGE SQUARE

CHOCOLATE SHORTBREAD TREAT

Will my dog go to heaven?

I think there are two questions here.

First, will there be dogs in heaven? I think so. God put a lot of effort into making them and I can easily imagine what a heaven for dogs would look like.

But there's another question, isn't there?

Will you have your dog in heaven? One thing we can be sure of is that because heaven is a perfect place where there is no more sadness or pain, you won't be standing there saying, "This is great but I really miss my dog!" So I think if you need your dog in order to be happy in heaven, then I'm sure he (or she) will be there.

Also, the absolutely best thing about heaven, something that is going to be more exciting and joyful than meeting up with any pet (or even any friend), is going to be meeting Jesus. That's why it's important to get to know him in this life. Even if we can't know for sure if our pets will go to heaven, God knows everything. He is perfect and good. So we can be sure he has a good plan for us and for our pets. When we go to heaven, we will be happy.

CHAPTER 6
HOW SHOULD I LIVE?

What does
God want me
to do with
my life?

This is a really important question.

The answer is that God wants us to know him, to love him and to serve him. That's three things and we need Jesus for each of them.

The Bible tells us about God's plan for us. We can come to know God through praying to Jesus; we can love God because he is like Jesus; and we can serve God because Jesus speaks to us and guides us. If we love God, we'll want to please him by making choices that make him happy. We can only know what choices to make by reading the Bible. As we read the Bible we get to know God and his ways, and as you follow Jesus then God has a plan for your life.

Remember, God only wants the best for you.

The important thing here is that prayer is something between you and God alone. It's a private conversation.

So by all means pray out loud with words if there is no one around. Otherwise pray in your head. It doesn't matter: God hears both types of prayer. But if you do pray in your head it's probably a good idea to still use words such as: "Dear Jesus, thank you for loving me . . . Thank you for all the good things I have and the people who look after me . . . (and you can name the people). I'm sorry for all the things I've done wrong, such as being nasty to my sister. And please help me to do this or not to do that."

The fact that we use words helps us to be clear in what we are saying. I sometimes find it helpful when praying to imagine that it is just God and me.

Whether you're praying aloud with others or praying alone, speak to your heavenly Father. He will always be listening and, even if you don't know what to say, he knows your heart and exactly what you mean.

Can every wrong thing be forgiven?

Where are the chocolates?

Ummm...

The brilliant and wonderful answer is yes. Now the idea that God forgives may seem hard to believe and, trust me, when you get older and see what people can do, it doesn't get any easier to believe. But God can forgive every wrong thing, both little ones and large ones.

When he was on Earth Jesus forgave many people and he hasn't changed; he still forgives today. Now the Bible teaches that Jesus doesn't just forgive everybody automatically; strange to say but some people don't want to be forgiven.

To be forgiven means that you have to come to Jesus, realising that he paid the price on the cross for the wrong things you've done. Then you have to say to him that you are sorry - and mean it - and promise that, with his power, you won't do whatever you did wrong again.

Sometimes it's very hard to believe that God forgives you. A really helpful thing the Bible says is that if we say we are sorry to God, and really mean it, he will completely forget what we did wrong and never remember it again.

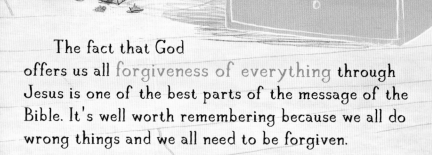

The fact that God offers us all forgiveness of everything through Jesus is one of the best parts of the message of the Bible. It's well worth remembering because we all do wrong things and we all need to be forgiven.

How can I know God?

This is the best question you can ask! Let me suggest three steps.

The first step is to know about Jesus. It's important to understand who Jesus is: that he was not just a good man, he was God who became one of us, he is God today, and he will rule for ever and ever. It's also important to understand what Jesus did: he showed us who God is and he died to pay the price for all the things that you and I have done wrong. And because of who Jesus is and what he did, we can pray to him. So that's the first step.

The second step is to pray to Jesus and say:

"Lord Jesus, I believe that you love me and died for me. Thank you. I'm sorry for all the things that I have done wrong. I want to follow you for the rest of my life. Come into my heart and change me into a better person."

And at the end of that prayer you can say "Amen" which means "I really mean what I say".

The third step is to follow Jesus. It's good to tell someone that you have made a decision to follow Jesus. Begin reading the Bible and start with one of the four Gospels - Matthew, Mark, Luke or John - in the New Testament. If it's at all possible, try to meet up with other people at a church who know and worship Jesus. And, every day, try to pray to Jesus and talk to him about all the good things and the hard things in your life. He would love to hear from you.

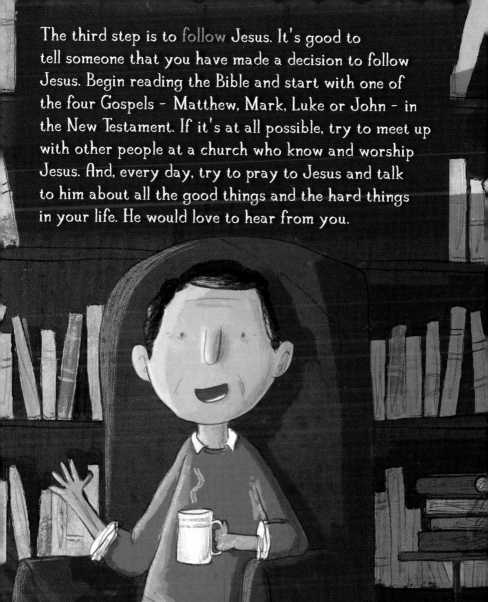

Copyright © 2019 J.John

Published in 2019 by Theology For Little People,
Philo Trust, Witton House, Lower Road,
Chorleywood, Rickmansworth, WD3 5LB,
United Kingdom.

www.canonjjohn.com

The right of J.John to be identified as the
author of this work has been asserted by him
in accordance with the Copyright, Designs and
Patents Act 1988.

All rights reserved. No part of this publication
may be reproduced or transmitted in any form
or by any means without prior permission in
writing from the publisher.

ISBN: 978-1-912326-04-4

All Scripture quotations are taken from the Holy Bible,
New Living Translation, copyright © 1996, 2004, 2007,
2013, 2015. Used by permission of Tyndale House
Publishers, Inc., Wheaton, Illinois 60189, USA.
All rights reserved.

Illustrated by Tom Tinn-Disbury, t.tinn.disbury@gmail.com
Design Management by Jeni Child, info@jenichild.com
Printed by Verité CM Ltd, www.veritecm.com

Goodbye